CREEPY CHRONICLES

Beyond the Grave

Written by Barbara Cox and Scott Forbes

Gareth Stevens
Publishing

CONTENTS

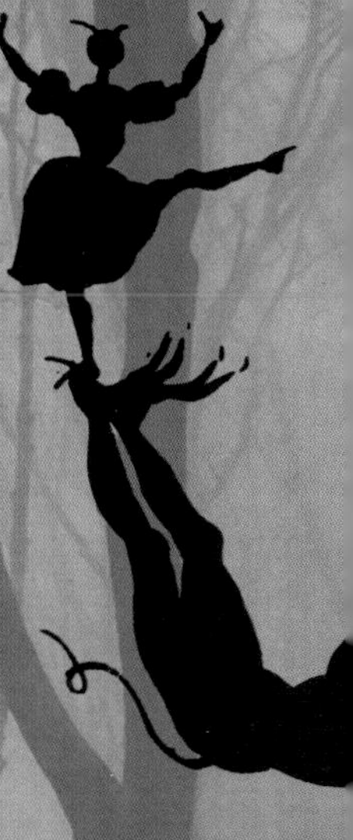

Trick or treat! The scariest night of the year is here. A perfect excuse for ghouls, demons, zombies, and creatures from the Underworld to come back from the dead and terrorize the living. And if that isn't enough to make you shiver with fear, there are screaming skulls, a headless horseman, grave robbers, and flesh eaters lurking in the darkness. But don't worry. If you disguise yourself well enough on Halloween, perhaps you'll be mistaken for one of these evil-doers and be fine. If not, you're at risk to lose more than just your costume. I hear zombies are particularly fond of brains . . .

BEYOND THE GRAVE

ZOMBIE

A ZOMBIE is a dead person that has been brought back to life. Through the use of magic, the Zombie can be made to walk around and do things, but it is not truly alive and is usually under the control of a magician. The idea of Zombies originated in the Voodoo religions of Africa and the Caribbean.

ZOMBIE

OTHER NAMES: Zonbi, nzumbe.

FACT OR FICTION: There are many stories of their existence. No genuine Zombies have ever been scientifically examined, though there are scientific theories about how "zombification" might actually happen.

DESCRIPTION: May look almost like a normal person or may be in a state of decay. Has a typically glazed or "hypnotized" stare. Moves slowly. Seldom speaks. Cannot feel pain.

WHERE THEY LIVE: Most common in Haiti, but also known to occur in other Caribbean islands and in West Africa and South Africa.

POWERS: Zombies do not possess any special magic powers, but they can terrify living people just by their appearance.

WEAKNESSES: Have no mind or will-power of their own and can act only in obedience to commands.

DIET: Zombies like to eat humans, especially brains. However, if a Zombie can be made to eat salt, that will make it return to its grave.

OTHER CHARACTERISTICS: Very popular in horror films and comics.

THE BOKOR

Most of the stories of Zombies in films and books have originated from Haitian legends. There is still a belief in Haiti that Zombies are possible and have existed.

A Zombie can only be created by a "bokor," a Voodoo magician who practices "magic of the left hand" or black magic. It is believed that, through the use of spells and drugs, the bokor captures a person's soul. The person quickly falls ill and dies. After they have been buried, the bokor raises the corpse from the dead and makes it his slave. As long as he keeps its soul, the Zombie has lost its personality and free will and can only act to carry out the bokor's commands. However, it is a dangerous creature since it feels no pain and cannot be killed, and the fear that it inspires makes sure that the bokor will get whatever he wants from the living.

Usually, the Zombie walks slowly and has a fixed stare. It may decay in the same way as a corpse in the grave, but it will keep walking and obeying the bokor's orders until it really falls apart, at which point the sorcerer may have to get a new one.

ZOMBIES IN AFRICA

The Zombie legends originate in Africa, where the Voodoo religion came from.

West Africa In West African tradition, the part of the soul that the bokor captures is called the Zombie Astral. It is believed that sorcerers keep a number of these spirits in glass jars and can use them for magical purposes. On payment of a fee, you can buy the influence of a Zombie Astral for good or evil purposes, though they lose their strength after a time.

South Africa In South African legends, Zombies may be dead or can be living people who have been taken over by a sorcerer and are kept in a trance-like state. They can be created by witches and even by children who are unaware of their own magic powers and can call up the dead without knowing it. A powerful witch doctor can break the spell.

There's a legend of the Zombie Train, which looks from a distance like a train full of people but is actually full of Zombies under the control of a witch. Unsuspecting living people who board the train at night are either flung off again into the desert, or are forced to join the Zombies as a slave laborer.

A SCIENTIFIC EXPLANATION FOR ZOMBIES?

In the 1980s, a Canadian scientist, Wade Davis, studied several cases of apparent real-life Zombies. He concluded that these people had never actually died, but had been drugged into a deep coma, declared dead, and buried. The bokor had then dug them up and revived them by administering further powerful drugs. From then on, they were kept in a permanently drugged state by the bokor; they also believed that they had died and were Zombies and so accepted their new life. The drugs included the powerful poison tetrodotoxin, extracted from the puffer fish, and the plant extract datura. Some of Davis's work has been questioned by other scientists, but it seems likely that the use of drugs, as well as forms of mental illness, would explain many of the Zombie legends.

MOVIE ZOMBIES

In most horror films about Zombies, there is no controlling sorcerer and the Zombies are an independent race of the undead with an overwhelming desire to eat living people, particularly the brains which are their favorite delicacy. People who are bitten by Zombies become Zombies themselves. This makes for more exciting stories, but is invented and not part of the original legend.

GHOUL

A creature that lives in graveyards and eats corpses.

It's not clear whether Ghouls start out as people and then become transformed into undead monsters through eating human flesh, or whether they are spirit beings to begin with. They are only seen at night so it's possible that daylight, and also fire, may harm them. They look a little human, but are very pale, long, and thin with long claw-like hands. They seem to haunt the same graveyards for centuries, so they are probably immortal. They like to go around in groups and seem to enjoy their grave-robbing work, since their laughter can be heard from a distance. Humans who enjoy stories about the misery of others are sometimes described as "ghoulish."

DOKKAEBI

Korean spirits can be kind or cruel, depending on how you behave.

A Dokkaebi in its natural state is roughly human-shaped with a red face, bulging eyes, and one or two horns on its head. It is covered in fur and carries a stick or club, which is really a magic wand. The chances of seeing a Dokkaebi looking like this are slim, because it has the ability to transform itself into anything at any time and has a hat that can make it invisible. It can also transform objects into other things using its club or wand.

These spirits are unpredictable and easily annoyed, but they're kind to good-hearted people. They tend to go out looking for trouble and will torment anyone they decide to pick on, though usually with good reason. They're ignorant and rough, and rather too fond of a drink, but like to give themselves praise and show off their magic powers.

Many Korean folktales tell of face-to-face encounters with Dokkaebi and even of people who became good friends with one. Mostly, they jump out at you in quiet places like graveyards and try to frighten or bully you, but it's possible to outsmart them.

Below: A Necromancer invokes a spirit.

NECROMANCER

A magician who specializes in summoning the spirits of the dead.

A Necromancer practices black magic, or more specifically, anything associated with death and usually involving rituals to summon and question the spirits of the dead. Necromancy is considered to be a particularly dangerous form of black magic, because it attempts to break down the barrier between the living and the dead—usually so that the Necromancer can gain information from the dead and therefore become more powerful himself.

The rituals of Necromancy are complicated and require a high level of magic knowledge. Parts of dead bodies are believed to be used in the rituals and so Necromancers often deal with Ghouls and other graveyard inhabitants.

GRAVE ROBBER

Someone who digs up graves and removes the contents in order to sell them.

Many people in past cultures were buried with their valuable belongings, for example, the ancient Egyptians, the Aztecs and Mayans of South America, and the Native Americans of North America. Throughout history, criminals have been known to dig up these graves and steal the precious artifacts to sell. Many believe that such treasure is cursed and that even archaeologists who take it to show in museums will suffer as a result.

CATACOMB

A CATACOMB is an underground burial chamber, usually very large and containing the remains of many dead people. Most catacombs, however, have been unused for a very long time. They have been used as meeting places for all kinds of people who want to keep out of the public eye—from smugglers to people interested in witchcraft.

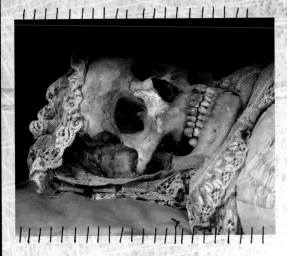

ROME CATACOMBS

The best-known and oldest catacombs are in Rome, Italy, where many people, including some of the earliest Popes, were buried. Other European cities later built catacombs. In a few places, they continued to be used until the twentieth century. In most countries, it became more common to bury the dead in cemeteries or in crypts under churches.

PARIS CATACOMBS

The catacombs that lie under the city of Paris, France, are an ossuary, or place where the skeletal remains of people are kept. Since the time of the ancient Romans, the remains of about six million people have been collected here.

THE SLEEPING DEAD

The process of decay is slower in a catacomb than for a burial in a grave, and coffins remain intact in catacombs for a very long time. There are a few catacombs, such as the one in Palermo, Sicily, in Italy, where the bodies have been embalmed and are not in coffins but on display in alcoves and on shelves, some sitting in chairs. There are about 8,000 dead, some still well preserved but others now reduced to skeletons.

Below: The catacombs in Rome, Italy.

Opposite: The catacombs in Palermo, Sicily, in Italy.

SCREAMING SKULL

The skull of a murder victim that cries out for vengeance.

There are many legends of screaming skulls. Usually, the skull belonged to someone who was murdered, but the murderer was never brought to justice. In some stories, the skull is accidentally dug up, and takes the opportunity to give the finder a scare by screaming at them and then demanding their help in getting revenge. There is a famous story of a screaming skull from Dorset in England, which is the skull of an African slave who asked to be buried in his native land, but whose wishes were not respected.

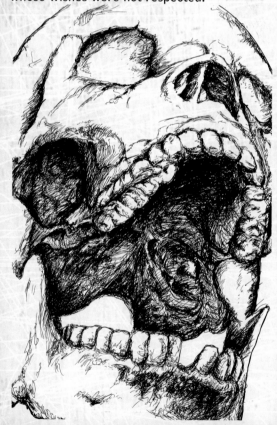

SKELETON WARRIOR

An undead skeletal fighter with an evil nature.

A Skeleton Warrior is similar to a Zombie, since it is raised from the dead by a powerful magician, who then controls it completely. However, as its name suggests, a Skeleton Warrior is an animated set of bones with all the flesh removed. These Warriors usually wear some form of armor to help keep their bones together, but, being undead, they are more or less indestructible.

Skeleton Warriors generally have very nasty natures, because the magic used to create them will only work on someone who, in life, was particularly evil-hearted.

It's really a bad idea to get into a fight with a Skeleton Warrior, unless you're a powerful magician yourself.

HEADLESS HORSEMAN

A headless ghost rider on a horse who brings a sense of impending doom.

Headless Horsemen appear all over the world in legends. They are very frightening and to see one is generally a sign that something bad is going to happen. Headless Horsemen often ride a grey horse and wear a long grey coat. Sometimes they carry their head tucked under their arm or propped on the saddle in front of them. In German legend, the Headless Horseman seeks out those who have gone unpunished for crimes.

In the folklore of Cornwall, England, a Horseman with half a face and half a head roams the moors looking for souls to steal.

There are many Headless Horseman stories in the United States. Most date back to the Civil War, but the most famous one appears in the story "The Legend of Sleepy Hollow" by Washington Irving (published 1820). This Horseman is supposedly a soldier whose head has been blown off by a cannonball during the American Revolution. Despite being buried in the graveyard of the peaceful small town of Sleepy Hollow, the Horseman cannot rest, but wanders at night, attacking the living. He even uses his head as a weapon, hurling it with tremendous force to strike down his victim.

HALLOWEEN

THE DATE OCTOBER 31 is traditionally a festival of the dead and all things ghostly. It is the day when spirits rise from their grave to wander the earth, and is their last chance before All Hallows' Eve (or All Saints' Day) to take revenge on the living. This is why people invented the custom of dressing up, or disguising themselves with masks and costumes, so the vengeful spirits wouldn't be able to recognize them!

ALL HALLOWS' EVE

The word Halloween was originally All Hallows' Eve, meaning the day before All Hallows' or All Saints' Day, which is on November 1. All Saints' is a particularly holy day for many Christians and is followed by All Souls' Day on November 2, when prayers are said for the dead and families visit the graves of their loved ones. So, in many parts of the world, this is a season when the lands of the dead and the living are less separated than usual, when the dead are remembered and respected and may come to visit their families and friends. In many countries, Halloween is considered to be the day when evil spirits are abroad, before the two holy days that renew the influence of good in the world.

Since Halloween is the last chance for restless spirits to wander the earth and take vengeance on the living, Halloween is definitely the night when anything evil—from demons to witches—will come out to play.

AUTUMN FESTIVAL

In northern countries, Halloween is very much an autumn festival and includes traditions to do with the food of the season, like apples (bobbing) and pumpkins (jack-o'-lanterns). In modern times, it has also become associated with dressing-up in costume as witches, wizards, and monsters of various kinds, holding parties, and "trick-or-treating," but this harmless fun should not make us forget the deeply spooky nature of Halloween.

ANCIENT ORIGINS

The ancient Celtic festival of Samhain was at about the same time as Halloween. It marked the end of the "lighter half" of the year and the beginning of the "darker half" and was also a festival of the harvest. It is believed that Samhain was the start of the New Year for ancient Celtic societies. Some of the Samhain rituals have been developed over the centuries into more modern festivities. For instance, bonfires were very important at Samhain, and these are now part of Halloween in many countries, while in England they're part of Guy Fawkes' or Firework Night (November 5). Masks and costumes were worn at Samhain to keep evil spirits away, and candles were lit and placed inside large hollowed-out turnips with faces carved on them—both of these traditions have survived into the modern Halloween, though now we use pumpkins to make the jack-o'-lantern with its eyes and toothy grin. Importantly, Samhain was believed to be the time when the dead could access the living world and when extra care must be taken to honor them and make them welcome if they chose to visit. Places might be set for the dead at a family's Samhain feast.

DRESSING UP

The ancient idea behind Halloween costumes was that, if you were masked and disguised, the evil spirits or unhappy ghosts wouldn't know who you were and couldn't harm you. If you dressed as a witch or ghost, they might even think you were one of their own kind. Most people have forgotten this original idea and now see Halloween as a chance to dress up as a character from a film or book series.

TRICK OR TREAT

This part of Halloween has long been popular in the United States and in recent years has been adopted in the United Kingdom and other countries too. Groups of children in Halloween costumes will go around their neighborhood knocking on doors and asking for a "treat," which will usually be candy. If the neighbor refuses, the children will play a mildly nasty "trick," such as throwing eggs at the house or something similar. "Trick or treat" seems to be a combination of two ancient traditions —the Scottish custom of guising, where children and young people wore costumes for Halloween, and the Northern English Mischief Night, which was usually in early November, when practical jokes of all kinds were played, especially by children.

DEMON

DEMON

OTHER NAMES: Devil, Fallen Angel, fiend, incubus, succubus, evil spirit.

FACT OR FICTION: Many people believe demons to be fact.

DESCRIPTION: Like the Devil, demons are often shown with horns, wings, and a tail and holding a forked trident, which looks a bit like a pitchfork. However, demons may take many forms and cultures around the world all have their own kinds of demons. Some demons may look like any normal human, but they may have hidden wings or a special mark on their body that shows they are not human but an evil demon. Demons can also take the form of beautiful women.

WHERE THEY LIVE: Demons can live anywhere, but obviously many prefer the dark and gloomy Underworld.

POWERS: Demons can be strong and fast, and many can also fly. Some are immune to flames or heat. They can play tricks on people's minds.

WEAKNESSES: Although demons cannot be killed, they can be banished if you know the right words to say.

DEMONS are evil spirits that are well known for tempting humans into behaving badly. Many people think that demons are a kind of angel that has gone bad, and they are often called "Fallen Angels." Like angels, demons may have wings, and many live in the Underworld and are immune to heat and fire.

FALLEN ANGELS

The original Greek word "daemon" means any kind of spirit, good or bad. The spelling "demon" is generally used to describe the very powerful evil beings that are believed by many religions to exist and to be at work on earth. Demons are based in the Underworld, away from the light of goodness, but can move amongst us and are always looking for ways to get more power over human beings and the world we live in.

Demons are the equals of angels, and many of them are thought to be angels who have "fallen," or become bad. They're mostly invisible to humans, but when they do appear they often have a fiery appearance, as well as being connected with darkness.

Demons are associated with temptation and with people's dangerous weaknesses.

Traditionally, demons like a challenge, so there are many stories of a saint or a holy person being picked out by a demon as a good target for temptation and having to battle to keep control of their soul.

SEVEN DEADLY DEMONS

People from different religions have attempted to classify and describe demons. One of the most famous Christian classifications lists the demons who are linked to the Seven Deadly Sins and who will try to tempt you to indulge:

Lucifer Demon of pride (though Lucifer is also used as a name for the Devil).

Mammon Demon of money and the love of money.

Asmodeus Demon of lust and passion.

Leviathan Demon of envy.

Beelzebub Demon of gluttony and greed.

Amon Demon of rage.

Belphegor Demon of sloth and idleness.

These demons, sometimes called the Princes of Hell, all have other evil work to do, but these particular sins are their areas of special interest.

CERBERUS

CERBERUS was a huge and terrifying dog who sat at the gates of the Underworld of ancient Greek mythology. He had three heads and was sometimes shown with a mane of live snakes and a snake for a tail.

GUARD DOG

Cerberus's task was to stop living people from entering the Underworld and to stop anyone at all from getting out. He was once kidnapped by Hercules who captured him as one of the "labors" or tasks that he had to fulfill to appease King Eurystheus. But Cerberus was so hideous that when Hercules triumphantly brought the dog to Eurystheus, he was told to take him straight back to the Underworld again.

ORPHEUS RESCUES EURYDICE

Orpheus, the legendary musician, was one of the few living people to get past Cerberus. He needed to get into the Underworld to rescue his beloved wife Eurydice. He lulled Cerberus to sleep with beautiful music and was able to plead with Hades, the god of the Underworld, to release Eurydice. Hades agreed, but only on condition that Orpheus let Eurydice follow him and didn't look back at her until both were above ground. The two of them passed the still-sleeping Cerberus and were nearly above ground when Orpheus looked back, and lost Eurydice forever.

HEL AND GARM

HEL is the goddess who rules Helheim. She decides how the dead are going to live through eternity in her realm. Garm is Hel's dog, who guards the entrance to the Underworld.

THE GATES OF HELHEIM

Helheim is the Underworld in Norse mythology. It's gloomy and contains many vast houses with very high walls. Not all the dead go there, only those who die of sickness or old age. Those who die bravely, for example in battle, go to Valhalla which is a much more cheerful place. Helheim is not the same as Hell. Hell is extremely hot and all the souls who go there are tortured, while in Helheim they mostly just lead a very sad and quiet life.

The ruler of Helheim, the goddess Hel, is tall, thin, dark, bony, and fierce. She can be merciless—when the god Baldr died and the other gods begged her to let him come back to the living, she said she would only do so if everyone on earth wept for him. One giant refused to weep and so Hel kept Baldr with her for eternity.

Hel's dog, Garm, looks like a huge hunting dog, but has four eyes and is always dripping with blood. It is said that the darkness of Helheim hangs about him.

HELLHOUND

A hound that comes and goes between the Underworld and the living world.

Unlike the guardians of the Underworld such as Cerberus and Garm, Hellhounds live in the Underworld but are free to roam in the world above, as big black dogs with red eyes who inspire terror in all human beings who see them.

Known all over the world, they may hunt in a pack, but they're most often seen alone in desolate places. Stories of Hellhounds are very ancient in Britain. One hound, called the Black Shuck, has been seen in the counties of Essex, Norfolk, and Suffolk since before even the Vikings came. Each time he appears, at least one person who sees him dies soon after. He once ran through a church, leaving scorch marks behind him, and two people who were praying dropped dead on the spot.

Left: Hellhound.
Above right: Fomorii.

FOMORII

Ancient Irish tribe, thought to come up from the Underworld.

The Fomorii or Fomorians lived on an island off the coast of Donegal and frequently attacked other tribes of ancient Ireland. They were violent and misshapen— sometimes described as having goats' heads or having one foot, one arm, and one eye— and were known to have access to Hell.

FURY

THE FURIES were terrifying and hideous goddesses of justice and revenge. Three sisters, they all had leathery wings, snakes for hair, and blood dripping from their eyes.

TOUGH BUT FAIR

The names of the three Furies, from ancient Greek mythology, were Megaera (the jealous one), Alecto (unceasing anger) and Tisiphone (avenger of murder). They were also known as the Daughters of the Night. Sometimes they lived in the Underworld, but mostly they were among the living, hunting down evil-doers.

The Furies would punish any crime, but especially offenses against the gods and crimes within the family such as violence towards a family member. The crime they hated most was the murder of a parent. They never gave up and would pursue offenders to the ends of the earth if necessary. Their favorite punishment was to make criminals go insane—in fact, knowing that the Furies were after them was enough to make most people go mad anyway.

However, the Furies were completely fair—they always knew the truth about any crime and would never punish anyone who was innocent. They could also defend the weak and would protect beggars, wanderers, and some animals.

HARPY

FLESH EATERS

Harpies were always hungry for flesh of any kind and would steal food, even from a king's table. The word "harpy" comes from a Greek word meaning "to grab" or "to snatch," and Harpies were famous for seizing people and taking them away to the Underworld, where they would torture them and tear them to pieces.

Unlike the Furies, the Harpies were not fair judges: they might drag you off to the Underworld on instructions from one of the gods. You might have committed a crime and deserved punishment—or you might just be unlucky. You could be innocent and they'd take you anyway because they were hungry.

Some legends say they were a living form of the harsh winter winds that cause destruction to anything that happens to be in their path. If people disappeared unexpectedly, it was thought that the Harpies might have taken them.

HARPIES were monsters from ancient Greek mythology. They were huge birds with the heads of (usually ugly) women and big sharp claws. They were vicious and permanently hungry and could take you to the Underworld.

DARK DWARF

The Dark Dwarves are ancient beings in mythology. They were formed from the maggots that ate the flesh of the great giant, Ymir, who was the first living thing to be created in the world, according to Norse legend. However, later they were given the gift of reason and became cunning. These Dwarves were clever craftsmen and made magical items for the gods, but they were considered untrustworthy and too fond of gold and treasure.

ONI

An Oni is a horned Japanese demon with big sharp teeth and appears in many legends. Onis often have red, green, or blue skin, and they always have horns, claws, and large, sharp, fang-like teeth. Oni dislike holly, which can be planted in your garden to keep them away from the house. It's best to keep them away, since they hunt for sinners to eat.

AMMUT

Known as the Devourer of the Dead, Ammut was a monster, part hippopotamus and part lion with the head of a crocodile. She waited in the Underworld when the hearts of the dead were being weighed. If the dead person's heart was not pure enough to be allowed into Heaven, then the heart would be given to Ammut to eat, and the person's soul must wander forever.

Right: Ammut was a female demon from Egyptian mythology.

GLOSSARY

Ancient: of or relating to a period of time long past

Archaeologist: a scientist that studies the life, tools, monuments, and remains left by ancient peoples

Artifact: a usually simple object showing human work and representing a culture or stage in the development of a culture

Bokor: a Voodoo magician who practices black magic

Celtic: of or relating to a characteristic of the Celts or their languages

Coma: a sleeplike state of unconsciousness

Corpse: a dead body

Crypt: an underground chamber for burial

Extract: to get out by pressing, distilling, or by a chemical process

Folklore: customs, beliefs, stories, and sayings of a people handed down from generation to generation

Guising: the Scottish custom of children disguised in costumes going house to house at Halloween

Hypnotize: to put someone into a trancelike state

Immortal: living forever

Immune: not influenced by something

Legend: a story coming down from the past whose truth is popularly accepted but cannot be checked

Mythology: a collection of myths dealing with the gods/goddesses of a particular people

Norse: the Scandanavian people

Ossuary: a place where the skeletal remains of people are kept

Sorcerer: a person who practices magic

Vengeance: punishment given in return for an injury or offense

Vengeful: wanting revenge

Please visit our website, www.garethstevens.com. For a free color catalog of all our high-quality books, call toll free 1-800-542-2595 or fax 1-877-542-2596.

Library of Congress Cataloging-in-Publication Data

Cox, Barbara.
Beyond the grave / by Barbara Cox and Scott Forbes.
  p. cm. — (Creepy chronicles)
Includes index.
ISBN 978-1-4824-0227-8 (pbk.)
ISBN 978-1-4824-0229-2 (6-pack)
ISBN 978-1-4824-0226-1 (library binding)
1. Supernatural — Juvenile literature. 2. Mythology — Juvenile literature. I. Title.
BF1461.C69 2014
133.1—dc23

First Edition

Published in 2014 by
Gareth Stevens Publishing
111 East 14th Street, Suite 349
New York, NY 10003

Produced for Gareth Stevens by Red Lemon Press Limited
Concept and Project Manager: Ariana Klepac
Designer: Emilia Toia
Design Assistant: Haylee Bruce
Picture Researcher: Ariana Klepac
Text: Scott Forbes (Forest, Castle, Desert), Barbara Cox (all other text)
Indexer: Trevor Matthews

Images: Every effort has been made to trace and contact the copyright holders prior to publication. If notified, the publisher undertakes to rectify any errors or omissions at the earliest opportunity.

Bridgeman Art Library: 2 tl and b, 3 tr, 11 tl in box, 20 tl and c, 24 tr in box, 25 t, 26 t, 27 t and bl in box.
Corbis: 13 tl in box, br in box, 16 tl, 17 t, 18 br in box, 19 b in box, 22 tl, 27 br.
Getty Images: 18 tl in box.
iStockphoto: other images as follows:
stick borders 6, 20; grim reaper 16; grunge borders 21, 22; hands 21, 22; cross stitches 22, 26, frames 24.
Martin Hargreaves: 23 t
Shutterstock: all other images

KEY: t = top, b = bottom, l = left, r = right, c = center

Printed in the United States of America

CPSIA compliance information: Batch #CW14GS: For further information contact Gareth Stevens, New York, New York at 1-800-542-2595.

Gareth Stevens
Publishing